So

by Sandra Fernández

 HOUGHTON MIFFLIN HARCOURT
School Publishers

PHOTOGRAPHY CREDITS: Cover © Jupiter Images, (i) © Alamy; 1 © Aflo/Corbis; 2 (tl) © Robert Michael/Corbis, (tr) © Alamy, (bl) © Alamy, (br) © JTPhoto/Brand X/Corbis; 3 © Alamy; 4 © Jerome Prevost/TempSport/Corbis; 5 © Jean-Yves Ruszniewski/TempSport; 6 © Aflo/Corbis; 7 © Duomo/Corbis; 8 © Image 100/Corbis; 9 © Image 100/Corbis; 10 © Alamy

Printed in China

ISBN-13: 978-0-547-42747-8
ISBN-10: 0-547-42747-6

2 3 4 5 6 7 8 0940 18 17 16 15 14 13 12 11 10

Soccer is a game that is loved around the world. Sisters and brothers play. Moms and dads play, too! Many people play soccer.

soccer ball   leg pads

You need a soccer ball
to play this sport.
Soccer shoes and leg pads
will keep you safe when
you play.

Two teams play this sport on a soccer <mark>field</mark>. The field is an open place that is covered with grass.
It has a net at both ends.

You move the ball down the field with your feet.
Using your head is okay, too!
But you cannot use your hands.

net

You score a goal
when you kick the ball
into the net.
Each goal is worth
one point.

Every team has a goalie. The goalie tries to keep the ball out of the net. The goalie is the ==only== player who can touch the ball with her hands.

referee

The referee runs up and
down the field.
He makes sure that
everyone plays safely
and by the rules.

The referee holds up a
card to show that
a player broke a rule.
Many players feel <mark>sorry</mark>
if they break a rule!

The team that scores the ==most== points wins. Players tell each other that they played well. They are good sports.

Responding

Word Builder

Soccer is played on a field.
What other games are played
on a field?

✏ **Write About It**

Text to Text Think of another
story about sports. Draw a
picture of a person playing the
sport. Label your picture. Use a
vocabulary word in your answer.

WORDS TO KNOW

brothers	**most**
everyone	**only**
field	**people**
loved	**sorry**

TARGET STRATEGY **Summarize**

Stop to tell important ideas as you read.